AF228750

AMAZING ANIMAL JOURNEYS

For the scientists and activists who dedicate their lives
to protecting animals and our planet.
Thank you.

AMAZING ANIMAL JOURNEYS

JENNIFER COSSINS

LOTHIAN
Children's Books

A Lothian Children's Book

Published in Australia and New Zealand in 2022
by Hachette Australia
Gadigal Country, Level 17, 207 Kent Street, Sydney NSW 2000
www.hachettechildrens.com.au

Hachette Australia acknowledges and pays our respects to the past, present and future Traditional Owners and Custodians of Country throughout Australia and recognises the continuation of cultural, spiritual and educational practices of Aboriginal and Torres Strait Islander peoples. Our head office is located on the lands of the Gadigal people of the Eora Nation.

A catalogue record for this book is available from the National Library of Australia

ISBN: 978 0 7344 2143 2 (hardback)

Designed by Kinart
Colour reproduction by Splitting Image
Printed in China by Asia Pacific Offset Limited

CONTENTS

INTRODUCTION

Animal migration is a fascinating phenomenon that has intrigued humans for centuries. Migrating animals move seasonally from one place to another in search of food, warmer weather or to breed. But how do they know where to go? How do they know when to leave? And how do they survive these risky journeys over thousands of kilometres?

When we think of migration, we might think of flocks of birds moving from north to south (and back again) to escape cold winters and find food in warmer parts of the world. But all sorts of animals migrate, including sea creatures like whales, mammals like antelopes and insects like butterflies. Many creatures migrate between northern and southern regions, while others journey from east to west, take complicated circular trips, or even vertical journeys up and down mountains.

If an animal doesn't migrate, it's because it doesn't need to. And this is lucky for them, as migration is often dangerous. Many animals face serious threats on their migration journeys – they can be targeted by predators or forced to navigate human-made obstacles such as busy roads.

For many animals, the instinct to migrate is triggered by changes in daylight, with longer days signalling summer is close, and shorter days warning that winter isn't far away. Some animals are also prompted by their hormones, as their reproductive cycles dictate where and when they should travel. For others, the urge to migrate is brought about by weather patterns, the lunar phases and water levels.

Some animals will stop off to eat along the way, but others have to prepare themselves for one long journey. This involves eating a lot in advance to build up their fat stores and, in some birds, even reducing the size of their internal organs to make them more flight efficient. Once they're on their way, animals use both visible and invisible cues to know where to go. Visible cues include natural landmarks, light patterns and, for those that travel at night, stars. Invisible cues include smells, tastes and even magnetic fields.

Whether they fly, swim or walk, migration is a truly remarkable feat and seeing some animals migrate is a breathtaking spectacle. In this book we'll discover 25 amazing animal journeys that will remind you just how extraordinary the world's animals are!

Check out the glossary on page 56 for some words you might not know.

ARCTIC TERN

The record for the longest migration of all the birds in the world belongs to the sun-loving Arctic tern. This bird migrates between the north and south poles in its never-ending search for sunlight.

The reason Arctic terns like summer so much is because 24-hour sunlight leads to an abundance of food in the polar regions. The terns spend the northern hemisphere's summer in large colonies spread out around the Arctic circle where they mate, raise their chicks and eat as much as they can. They leave in July or August, taking around three months to arrive in Antarctica by November, just in time for the southern hemisphere's summer. In February or March, they take off once again and head north.

The small Arctic tern is perfectly built for this extreme lifestyle. They are about 30 centimetres long, with narrow wings and short bodies, which make them very light. This lightness helps them take advantage of the ocean breezes, gliding long distances without having to use energy flapping their wings. They can even sleep and eat while gliding effortlessly through the skies.

Arctic terns cover a distance of around 30 000 kilometres with every round-trip migration, but because they don't fly in a straight line they can actually fly as much as 90 000 kilometres in a year. A true wanderer, these elegant terns are one of only a few animals on the planet that can be seen on every continent.

WILDEBEEST

Wildebeest, or gnu, are an antelope species with large heads and curved horns. Between December and April, they are found across the southern plains of the Serengeti National Park in Tanzania, East Africa, where they give birth to their calves. Around half a million calves are born each year.

In May or June, when the rainy season ends, the wildebeest gather and begin to move north on the hunt for fresh grass and water. About 1.5 million wildebeest make up the herd, and they are joined by several other animals, such as zebras and gazelles. Together, they follow an enormous clockwise circuit hundreds of kilometres long known as the Great Migration.

The yearly journey is packed with danger. The large size of the herd provides some safety, but thousands of wildebeest still die. Any struggling members of the herd, often the very young or very old, are targeted by predators such as lions or hyenas.

By July, the herd meets its biggest obstacle: the crocodile-infested Mara River. This crossing can be as spectacular as it is risky, as the wildebeest attempt to cross the gushing water in panic and confusion. Many wildebeest are lost to the choppy waters, fall victim to the hungry crocodiles or are taken by the lions that patrol the riverbanks, looking out for an easy meal of injured, weak or slow animals.

Around September, the herd heads east and must face the Mara River once more on their circular journey. They turn south in November, returning to plains full of fresh grasses, ready for another season of feeding and birthing.

The Great Migration is one of the largest mammal migrations on Earth. It is so large it can be seen from space.

PACIFIC BLUEFIN TUNA

The large, aggressive Pacific bluefin tuna usually grows to around 1.5 metres long and weighs around 60 kilograms, though much larger ones have been seen. The largest reported Pacific bluefin was three metres long and a whopping 450 kilograms!

Pacific bluefins spawn in the Sea of Japan or the north-western Philippine Sea, with the females producing between five million and 25 million eggs each. At around one year old, the little tuna embark on their biggest journey – an 8000-kilometre expedition across the Pacific Ocean to the coast of North America.

The journey is a long way for a young fish, but the tuna are super-fast — shaped for speed, they tuck in their fins and zip through the water at speeds of over 65 kilometres per hour.

Tuna are one of only a few warm-blooded fish, which means they can cope with the icy cold waters in the north Pacific Ocean just as well as the tropical waters of Mexico.

Once they reach the coast, the tuna will spend several years travelling up and down the coasts of Mexico and California, eating as much as they can and growing into the large predators they were born to be. At around seven years old, the tuna are fully grown. They cross the ocean again, returning to the region where they were born in order to reproduce.

After these two big migrations from one side of the Pacific Ocean to the other, the tuna tend to roam the western Pacific for the rest of their lives.

CHRISTMAS ISLAND RED CRAB

One of the most incredible migrations on Earth belongs to the Christmas Island red crab. Christmas Island sits in the Indian Ocean about 380 kilometres south of Java, Indonesia. Once a year, millions of red crabs emerge from the island's forests in a synchronised swarm, marching for the shore with unstoppable determination.

These bright-coloured crabs, whose bodies grow to about 12 centimetres wide, dislike sunlight and spend most of their lives tucked away in burrows deep in the forests. Around October or November, the first rain of the wet season prompts the crabs' migration to the ocean to mate and spawn.

It's a dangerous journey for the crabs, so local communities have built crab bridges and tunnels, and sometimes even close roads, to help them safely reach the ocean.

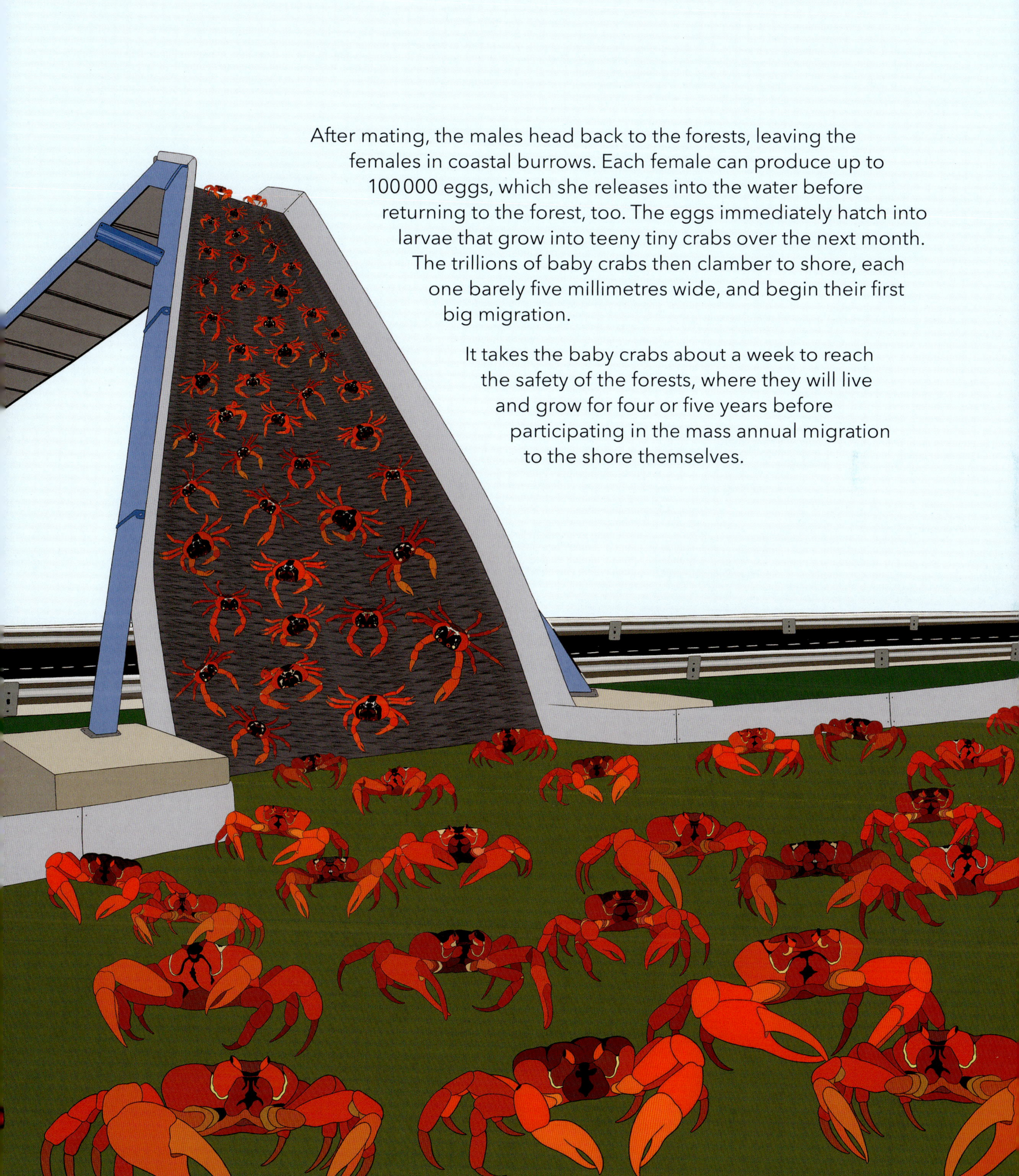

After mating, the males head back to the forests, leaving the females in coastal burrows. Each female can produce up to 100 000 eggs, which she releases into the water before returning to the forest, too. The eggs immediately hatch into larvae that grow into teeny tiny crabs over the next month. The trillions of baby crabs then clamber to shore, each one barely five millimetres wide, and begin their first big migration.

It takes the baby crabs about a week to reach the safety of the forests, where they will live and grow for four or five years before participating in the mass annual migration to the shore themselves.

BLACK-NECKED CRANE

The elegant and endangered black-necked crane is the world's only alpine crane species. Like their alpine goose friends the bar-headed geese (on page 24), black-necked cranes can fly at very high altitudes, allowing them to soar over the Himalayas when migrating.

In summer, they are found in wetlands high in the Himalayas. Like many crane species, black-necked cranes form long-lasting pairs and perform impressive and beautiful dances for each other during mating season. When breeding, the cranes are very territorial and will fiercely chase away fellow cranes. They don't mind other species, though, and can sometimes be seen sharing a nesting site with bar-headed geese.

Every year as the weather cools in October, 10 000 black-necked cranes migrate south to spend the winter in sheltered valleys at lower altitudes. Most of the population stays close to the Himalayan mountains, but a few adventurous cranes fly further, wintering in Bhutan, India and even as far away as Vietnam. Their return trip to the northern nesting grounds in late March takes up to a week.

One particular flock of black-necked cranes announces its arrival and departure in Bhutan by looping over the Gangtey Monastery three times every single year!

HUMPBACK WHALE

Known for their haunting songs and acrobatic displays, the huge humpback whale is found in every ocean on the planet.

Though they are about half the size of a blue whale, humpbacks are still enormous, growing up to 18 metres long and weighing about 40 tonnes — that's more than five African elephants put together! Their flippers are the longest limbs of any animal, growing up to five metres long. Like most whales, the female humpback is larger than the male.

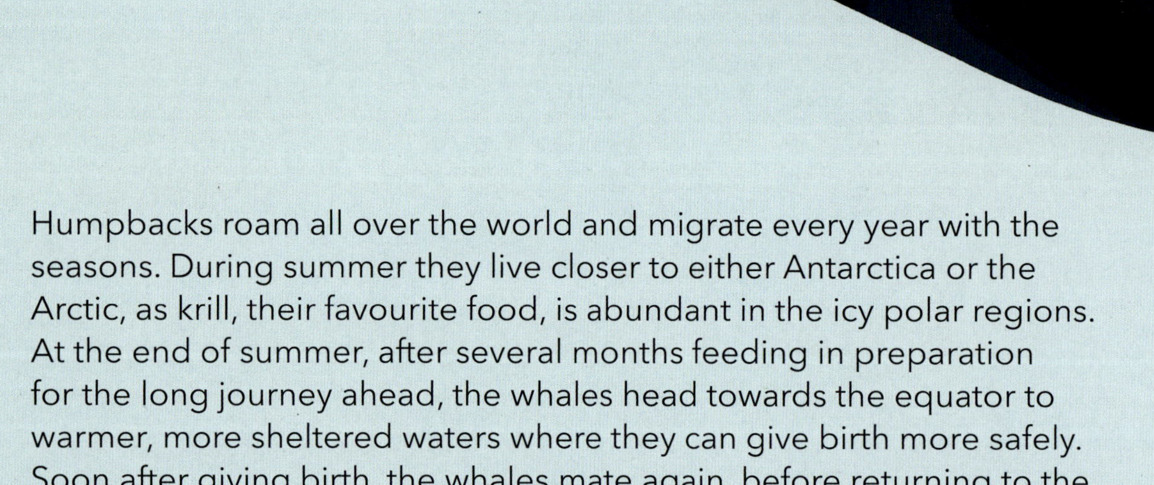

Humpbacks roam all over the world and migrate every year with the seasons. During summer they live closer to either Antarctica or the Arctic, as krill, their favourite food, is abundant in the icy polar regions. At the end of summer, after several months feeding in preparation for the long journey ahead, the whales head towards the equator to warmer, more sheltered waters where they can give birth more safely. Soon after giving birth, the whales mate again, before returning to the polar regions for summer.

These gentle giants of the sea have one of the longest migrations of any mammal, travelling about 8000 kilometres a year. But they don't rush the journey.

Humpbacks swim slowly while migrating, travelling only one or two kilometres an hour as they regularly rest, socialise, sing and play along the way.

STRAW-COLOURED FRUIT BAT

Straw-coloured fruit bats live in Sub-Saharan Africa and get their name from their yellowish fur. At 14–23 centimetres long and with a wingspan of up to one metre, they are quite large for a bat. In fact, they are the second-largest fruit bat found in Africa.

A highly social and noisy species, straw-coloured fruit bats form colonies of up to 100 bats. Once a year, between October and December, the bats flock together in their millions and fly thousands of kilometres to end up in one swampy forest in Zambia.

The fruit bats crowd into part of the Kasanka National Park, enticed by the abundant wild fruit that grows there after the first rains of the season. This epic feast is the largest gathering of mammals in the world, with more than eight million bats taking over a patch of forest no bigger than a football field.

By day, the bats roost, tightly packed, in the trees, bending branches under their weight as they sleep, rest and groom themselves. Then, at night, the forest comes alive with movement as the bats gorge on the plentiful fruits and flowers.

Every night is a feeding frenzy, with each bat eating around twice its body weight in fruit to build up energy reserves for the journey back.

The hungry bats stay in the park, guzzling fruit, until early January, when they begin the migration back to their home territories. This annual feast keeps the forest healthy and happy for another year, as the millions of bats help pollinate the forest's plants and spread seeds.

CARIBOU

The magnificent caribou have roamed the Arctic tundra of Canada and Alaska for many thousands of years. While they are technically the same species as the reindeers of Europe, caribou have never been domesticated and are taller and leaner than reindeer. They have adapted perfectly for long, arduous hikes in the Arctic wilderness and are constantly on the move in order to survive the harsh climate.

Caribou gather in massive herds of hundreds and, at times, thousands, travelling 1000–1350 kilometres every year over well-worn routes. The migration begins in spring when the caribou herds head to their remote birthing grounds in the far north where food is plentiful and the number of predators, such as wolves, bears and eagles, is low. Caribou calves are surprisingly small but are able to walk within 30 minutes of being born, which is a good thing as the herds don't linger.

In June, the caribou head further into the freezing north to escape the summer mosquitos that plague the tundra. Later, as summer draws to a close, they travel back southwards to avoid the worst months of the Arctic winter.

The round trip takes most of the year to complete and is believed to be the longest land migration on the planet.

It's a tough journey through some of the harshest weather conditions and often dangerous, with packs of hungry wolves seeking a young, old or weak caribou to feast on. As more roads are built and remote areas become increasingly developed, the caribou are faced with yet more challenges to their migration routes.

SWIFT PARROT

This aptly named bird is the world's fastest parrot, and one of only three parrots on Earth that migrate. Along with the orange-bellied parrot, swift parrots only breed on the island of Tasmania, where habitat loss is making survival increasingly difficult. The swift parrot is critically endangered, with as few as 750 of them left in the wild.

Swift parrots spend most of the year in north and south-east Tasmania, where they search out the best tree hollows for nesting and breeding, and the tastiest flowering gums for eating. At the end of summer, swift parrot chicks leave the nest and, accompanied by their parents, fly across Tasmania in small, noisy flocks.

By April, it's time for the biggest journey of their lives — crossing the 250-kilometre-wide Bass Strait, which they fly over in one non-stop trip that takes around five hours. Once they reach the mainland of Australia, these parrots are fairly nomadic, travelling around the south-eastern parts of the country looking for blue gum trees to feast on, mostly in Victoria and New South Wales.

Around September, the swift parrots head home to Tasmania for another summer of breeding and munching on the sweet nectar of the flowering Tasmanian blue gums.

ZEBRA

Thousands of zebras join the Great Migration (on page 4) in East Africa every year, but two smaller groups undertake their own mass migrations further south. These zebras spend the driest months of the year, from May to November, in the river lands of north Botswana or just over the border in Namibia, where there's plenty of water even in the dry season. Then, in December, up to 30 000 of them come together to begin their journey south, prompted by the rains that mark the beginning of the wet season. In a jumble of black and white, the throng of migrating zebras is a dramatic sight, kicking up dust as they travel in search of fresh grazing land.

The zebras head south in two different ways, with the largest herd trekking across the dry and barren Kalahari Desert to reach the Makgadikgadi Salt Pans. After the rains, this area is bursting with fresh, tasty grasses.

The other herd is a smaller group of just a few thousand Burchell's zebras, a sub-species of the plains zebra that is most common in Africa. This herd travels south from the Chobe River floodplains to the Nxai Pan National Park and back again, a journey of around 500 kilometres in total.

Whichever route they take, the zebras spend the rest of the wet season spread out over the grassy plains before gathering once more at the end of March to return to the more reliable water supply in the north.

MONARCH BUTTERFLY

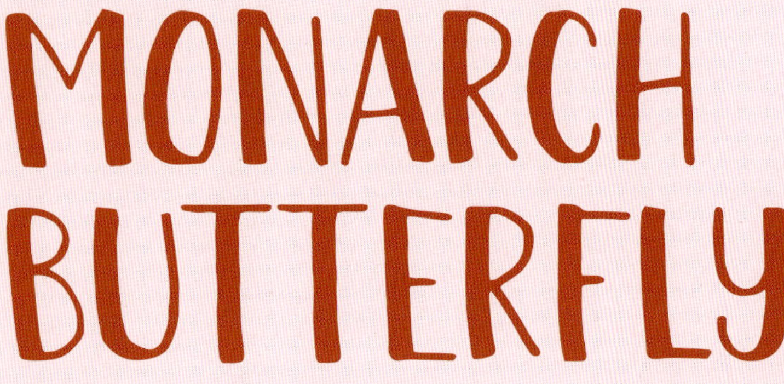

Monarchs are quite large for a butterfly, averaging around 10 centimetres in wingspan. They live all over the world, except in polar regions, but it's the North American monarchs that take the migration crown.

These monarchs spend summer in Canada and the northern regions of the United States before abandoning their homes in search of a warmer place to spend the winter. They fly over 3000 kilometres to the mountains of Central Mexico, where millions of them hibernate together on the branches of oyamel fir trees.

In spring, the butterflies head back north, but only for a short distance, to find a patch of milkweed plants. After laying 300–500 eggs, these butterflies die. When the next generation hatches into caterpillars, they eat lots of milkweed before forming a chrysalis and becoming adult butterflies. This process takes about a month.

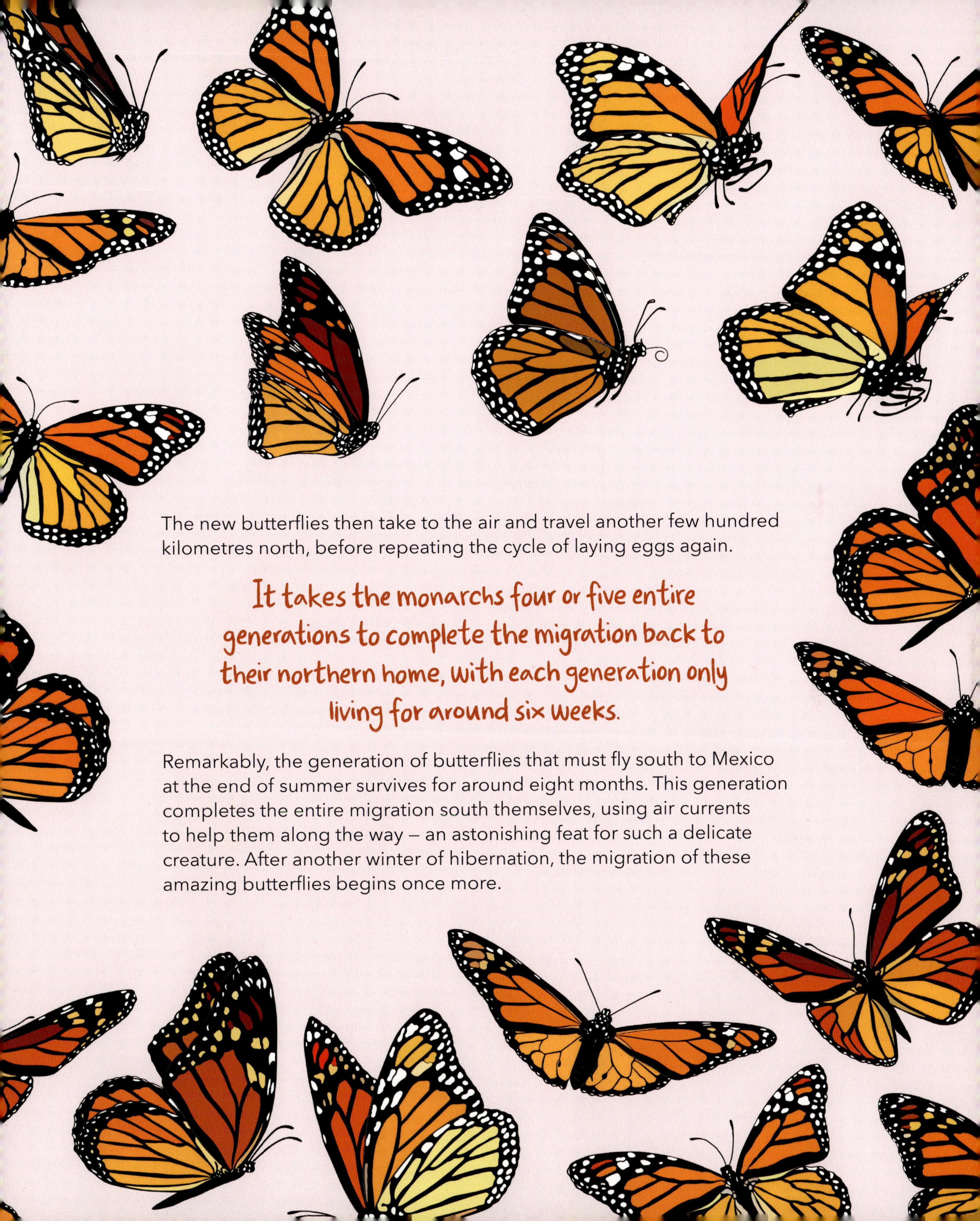

The new butterflies then take to the air and travel another few hundred kilometres north, before repeating the cycle of laying eggs again.

It takes the monarchs four or five entire generations to complete the migration back to their northern home, with each generation only living for around six weeks.

Remarkably, the generation of butterflies that must fly south to Mexico at the end of summer survives for around eight months. This generation completes the entire migration south themselves, using air currents to help them along the way — an astonishing feat for such a delicate creature. After another winter of hibernation, the migration of these amazing butterflies begins once more.

BAR-HEADED GOOSE

The impressive bar-headed goose flies higher than any other migratory bird, soaring through the Himalayas twice every year on its migration.

In the summer months, bar-headed geese live in the high-altitude lakes of Central Asia, but every year they migrate south to escape the cold, harsh conditions of the mountains in winter. These hardy birds can migrate over 1500 kilometres in a day and can fly at speeds of up to 80 kilometres per hour. Sometimes they fly for over 16 hours without a break.

Unable to glide, bar-headed geese must constantly flap their large wings, which generates a lot of body heat. Combined with their super-warm feathers and unusual natural resistance to extreme temperatures, this body heat stops ice from forming on their wings when they fly so high.

Bar-headed geese have greater lung capacity, stronger hearts and more red blood cells than other geese. This allows them to absorb more oxygen with each breath than other birds, which is another biological feature that helps keep them safe at high altitudes.

The height these geese can reach is mind-blowing — they have been seen flying over Mount Everest, which is the world's tallest mountain at 8849 metres high.

SOCKEYE SALMON

Many salmon species complete dramatic migrations from the ocean to their upstream spawning grounds, but the sockeye salmon is perhaps the most spectacular of all thanks to its strange colour-changing ways.

Sockeye salmon are native to the western coast of North America. They are born in freshwater lakes and spend the first few years of their lives there. They then journey out to the north Pacific Ocean where they swim vast distances, eating and growing, for several years. At this stage of their lives, sockeye salmon are silvery-coloured with fine black speckles and a blue-tinged back.

When it's time to breed, sockeyes migrate from the ocean back to freshwater rivers. The journey is not an easy one, with many salmon travelling over 1000 kilometres against the current, jumping over obstacles like large rocks and even small waterfalls along the way.

As they swim upstream, the sockeyes' bodies turn bright red and their heads an olive green. The males also change shape, developing a humped back and hooked jaws full of lots of tiny teeth.

Guided by smell, most sockeyes return to the same area where they were born. When they finally make it, the females lay up to 4500 eggs, often within metres of their own birthplace, and then search for the most attractive-looking male to fertilise them.

Sockeye salmon only get to breed once in their lives and afterwards both parents die, leaving the eggs alone to hatch, grow and become migrating sockeye salmon themselves.

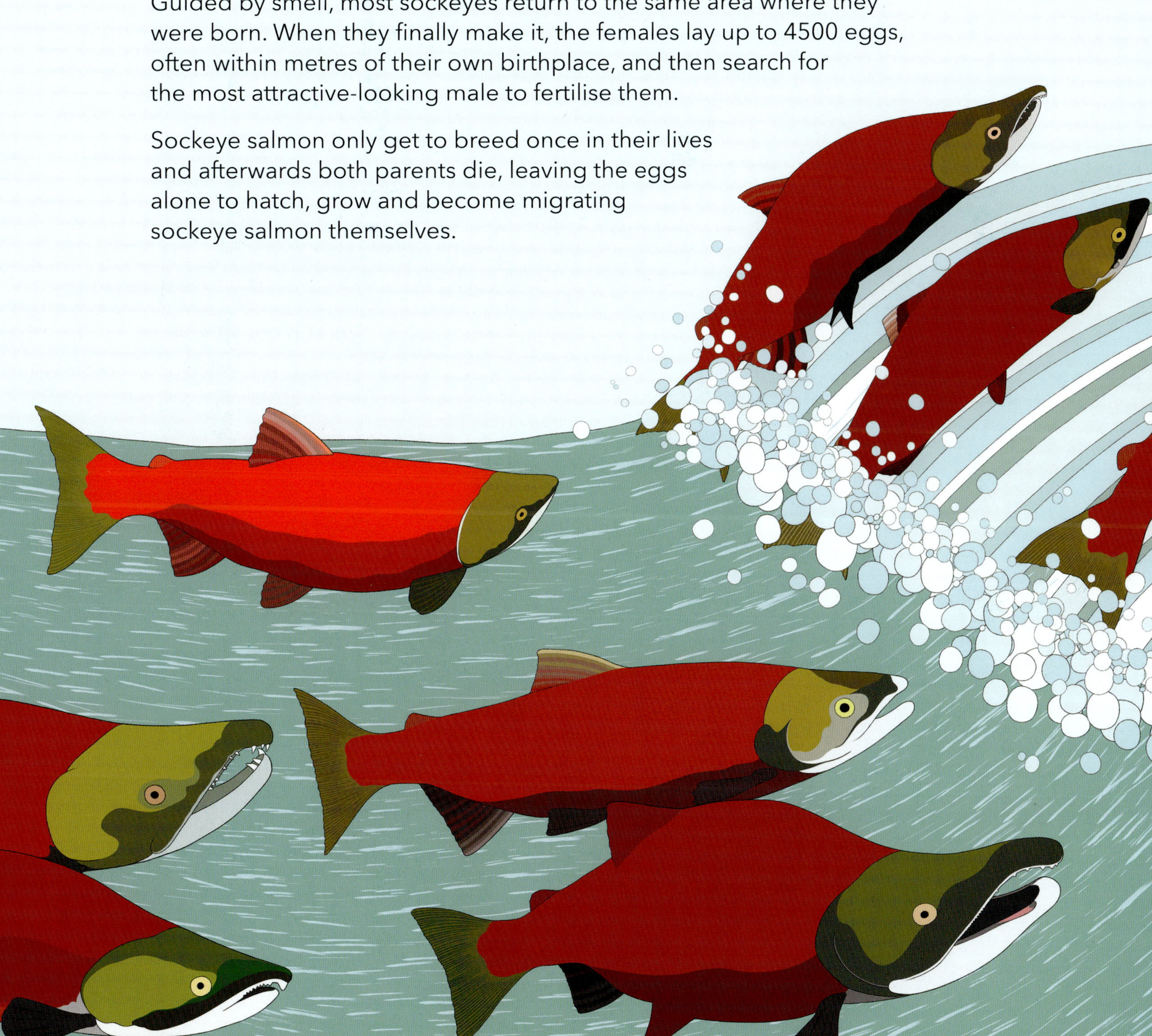

COMMON CUCKOO

The common cuckoo is anything but common – it's a crafty, clever bird with a migration story that conquers continents and oceans alike.

This widespread bird spends summers in Europe and Asia, where it breeds and lays its eggs, before it flies to Central Africa for warmer winters. Cuckoo parents don't have to wait for their young to grow before they migrate – they leave their young in the care of other birds instead.

A female cuckoo will find another bird's nest, remove one of the eggs and lay her own. She can even lay an egg that blends in, making it spotty or solid in colour depending on the host bird's eggs, so the host bird won't know they've been tricked.

Once hatched, the trickery continues, with the baby cuckoo often kicking the other chicks out of the nest so it can have all the food supplied by the foster parents. The cuckoo chick stays with its foster parents for a month or so after hatching, before leaving to migrate.

The cuckoos' migration route is one of the world's longest, with one cuckoo from Mongolia clocking up an incredible 12 000 kilometres on the journey to Central Africa, crossing the Indian Ocean as well as 16 countries. The round trip is one of the longest ever recorded for a land bird.

Common cuckoos flying from Europe have a slightly easier journey, but crossing the Sahara poses its own challenges as both oceans and deserts require a great deal of stamina to fly across without stopping.

WHITE-EARED KOB

The graceful white-eared kob is a species of medium-sized antelope that grows to about a metre tall.

During the dry season, hundreds of thousands of white-eared kob can be found in South Sudan's Sudd wetland, spread across the area in small groups that return to the same feeding and breeding sites year after year.

The Sudd is one of the largest tropical wetlands on the planet and one of Africa's greatest wildlife refuges, home to hundreds of bird species as well as elephants, tiang antelopes and many more mammals. However, this region is prone to flooding, so when the rains arrive it's time for many of its inhabitants to seek somewhere a little drier.

The massive herd of white-eared kob are joined by thousands of tiang antelopes, Mongalla gazelles, a few reedbuck antelopes and even some ostriches to undertake an epic journey south. This annual migration forms one of the biggest concentration of mammals on Earth, rivalling the wildebeest's Great Migration (on page 4) in size.

Tightly packed, the herd of around 1.2 million animals can stretch 80 kilometres long and up to 50 kilometres wide.

Each year, the herd travels as far as 1500 kilometres in search of less soggy land and fresh, nutritious grasses and reeds, before returning north for the dry season once more.

BAR-TAILED GODWIT

The bar-tailed godwit is a large wading bird that migrates each year from its northern breeding grounds, mostly in Alaska, all the way across the Atlantic Ocean to Australia and New Zealand. This is an incredibly long journey of over 11 000 kilometres, which takes the bar-tailed godwit around eight or nine days.

Unlike most birds, which stop to feed and rest many times along their migration routes, the bar-tailed godwit likes to fly long-haul. In fact, the bar-tailed godwit is a migration champion and currently holds the record for the longest non-stop migration of any bird.

The birds arrive in Australia and New Zealand in August. When returning to Alaska in mid-March, they usually complete their migration in two stages and take a longer route. The first non-stop stretch from Australia to the Yellow Sea, between China and Korea, is a huge flight of around 10 000 kilometres and takes about seven days. After a few weeks of feeding and resting to get their strength back, the bar-tailed godwits continue another 7000 kilometres to their Alaskan breeding grounds where they spend the northern summer.

In order to do such long flights, the bar-tailed godwit must undertake serious preparation. Like many animals, this means eating a lot in the weeks and months before migration. Over half their body weight is taken up by reserves of fat. These clever birds can also shrink some of their organs – the ones not needed for flying, like their stomach – to make room for fat and muscle.

GLOBE SKIMMER DRAGONFLY

Many species of dragonfly migrate, but the globe skimmer, as its name suggests, has the most extensive journey of all. An average-sized dragonfly – 4.5 centimetres long with a wingspan of around eight centimetres – the globe skimmer makes up for its lack of size with its incredible flying abilities.

Globe skimmers are found on every continent except for Antarctica. They are thought to be the highest-flying dragonflies, having been spotted flying over 6000 metres high in the Himalayas. As warm-weather lovers, though, they are generally found in places with an average temperature of around 20 degrees Celsius.

Globe skimmers can fly over 3000 kilometres without touching land, one of the longest insect flights known.

Each year, globe skimmers make a migration of over 18 000 kilometres, mostly in large, wandering loops around Africa and India following the monsoon season. They constantly chase their favourite warm, humid weather, searching for good ponds and puddles to spawn in. Like the migratory monarch butterfly (on page 22), several generations of these dazzling dragonflies are required to complete the full annual migration.

Most dragonflies spend up to a year living as larvae underwater, but as globe skimmers like to breed in temporary water sources, like puddles, they don't have time for such a relaxed childhood. Instead, they emerge from the water in just five or six weeks, ready to take on the world in search of their own special puddle.

ANDEAN FLAMINGO

Falsely associated with palm trees and tropical beaches, flamingos often inhabit some of the most inhospitable places on Earth. The Andean flamingo, the world's tallest and rarest species of flamingo, is one such example.

These striking birds spend their summers at high altitudes in the many salt lakes and lagoons of the Andes Mountains in South America. As social creatures, they form huge flocks of many thousands of birds.

Summer is breeding season and these beautiful birds know how to put on a show. The males often team up and perform in large groups, saluting their wings and even moving in unison to impress the females. Once they've formed monogamous pairs, the flamingos breed and work together to build a mud nest in the shallow water of the mountains' salt lakes. Both parents incubate the egg then raise the chick, and both male and female flamingos can produce a substance called crop milk, which they feed to their chicks until they are about two months old.

As the icy mountain winter approaches, the Andean flamingos' food becomes scarce and huge flocks migrate together to lower ground. But due the to habitat loss and water contamination from farming and mining, these flamingos are an endangered species. There are only around 34 000 left in the wild.

SAIGA ANTELOPE

The rare saiga antelope has an unusual nose, a strange up-down running style and is about the size of a goat. It may look awkward, but the saiga is perfectly designed for life in the arid, windswept plains of Central Asia and southern Russia. Their robust bodies and long, spindly legs provide them with the speed and endurance they need to survive in the harsh, semi-desert landscape. Their flexible noses filter out the clouds of desert dust that rise in the dry summers while also warming up the freezing air in winter before it hits their lungs.

In spring, saiga come together in a massive herd to migrate to their northern breeding areas. They then spend the summer in smaller groups, before gathering again to journey southwards to a warmer climate for the winter. The journey's length and route vary from year to year, depending on the weather and the availability of food, but it can be as long as 500 kilometres each way.

The saiga population once numbered in the millions, but it has declined by more than 95 per cent in recent years – the fastest known decline of any mammal. One of the main threats saiga face is poaching for their horns, which are as valuable on the black market as rhinoceros horns.

Saiga are also under threat from climate change, as drought becomes increasingly common, and from humans encroaching on their habitat for farming and fossil fuel production. These wandering migrants like to cross borders on their travels, and the increasing number of roads and border fences has also contributed to unsettling their journey.

EMPEROR PENGUIN

Emperor penguins undertake a short but impressive migration each year in March, travelling 100–150 kilometres over the Antarctic ice from their coastal feeding grounds to their inland breeding sites.

Emperor penguins are the largest penguin and grow to be over a metre tall. They mate for life and return to the same place every year to breed. After the tough, icy journey inland, the females lay a single egg, pass it to their partners, and then leave immediately to return to the ocean to feed. For the next four months, the fathers balance the eggs on their feet, unable to eat or drink, huddling in close with the other males to survive the long, dark and freezing Antarctic winter.

The eggs begin to hatch just as winter ends. The females return too, with bellies full of fish to feed the newborn chicks. With their partners home, the hungry males head off to the ocean for their own meals.

For the next few months, both parents take it in turns to forage in the sea and travel inland to look after the chicks, until the chicks are old enough to head out to sea by themselves.

This journey can be harrowing for the large but clumsy chicks, and they must fend for themselves in the face of predators such as sea birds and leopard seals. For four years, the emperor chicks will stay at sea, swimming, feeding and growing until they are fully grown and ready to migrate inland to breed, just like their parents.

GREAT SNIPE

Superstar flyer the great snipe is the fastest migratory bird on the planet! There are faster birds, as well as birds that fly longer distances, but the great snipe travels fast *and* far, covering distances of over 6500 kilometres non-stop at speeds of almost 100 kilometres per hour.

Another unusual feature of the great snipes' flying prowess is that they sometimes reach incredible heights, possibly challenging the bar-headed goose (on page 24) for the migration height record. Great snipes have been observed flying at an altitude of over 8000 metres, almost as high as Mount Everest.

Great snipes can travel all the way from their breeding grounds in Sweden to Africa in three days without stopping to eat, drink or sleep.

Most birds that fly such long distances without stopping do so because they are crossing an ocean and have no choice. But the great snipes' southern migration route is almost entirely over land, giving them plenty of opportunities to stop for a rest and a snack. For unknown reasons, these tough wading birds prefer flying 7000 kilometres from Sweden to Africa's Sahel region in one go.

Before leaving, great snipes almost double their body weight to ensure they have enough energy reserves to reach their destination.

After a month in the Sahel region, great snipes fly a further 2000 kilometres to their wintering grounds in Sub-Saharan Africa. At the end of winter they head north, but this time they don't need to bulk up as they make several stops along the way to rest and feed.

NEW ZEALAND LONGFIN EEL

The largest freshwater eels in the world, longfin eels can grow up to two metres long, weigh 20 kilograms or more, and can live to 80 years old. They grow slowly and spend almost all their lives in the alpine lakes and rivers of New Zealand before undertaking one of the world's most epic once-in-a-lifetime migrations.

When a longfin eel is ready to breed, it swims downstream and out to the ocean, transforming from a freshwater eel to a saltwater eel. It then swims thousands of kilometres north until it reaches tropical Pacific waters, where it spawns and almost immediately dies, leaving its eggs floating in the ocean.

The eggs hatch into larvae that spend the next year or so drifting back to New Zealand on the ocean current, although scientists have not yet been able to record their movements accurately. When the larvae reach the New Zealand coast, they grow into tiny transparent eels known as glass eels. The glass eels then swim into rivers, where they develop darker colouring, becoming young eels that are known as elvers.

The elvers begin a long journey, slowly growing while swimming further and further upstream each year, until they finally reach the alpine lakes and rivers they will call home.

Longfin eels must navigate waterfalls and climb dams, which they conquer with their unique climbing abilities.

When they eventually reach a good home, the eels stay there until their own lives are almost over and it's time to migrate, breed and die just as their parents did many years before.

RUFOUS HUMMINGBIRD

Not all hummingbirds migrate, but of those that do, the feisty rufous hummingbird has the longest journey. This tiny hummingbird can travel over 6000 kilometres on its annual migration — an impressive feat for a bird that, on average, is about 8 centimetres long and only weighs 3.5 grams. That's lighter than a 20 cent coin!

In relation to its size, this might just be the longest journey in the world, as the rufous hummingbird travels around 78 million times its body length one way.

Known for being fiercely territorial, these brightly coloured hummingbirds live almost exclusively in the western half of North America and migrate between Alaska and southern Mexico. Unlike many birds, hummingbirds migrate alone.

They leave their winter homes in Mexico in January and travel up the coast over several months to arrive at their northern summer residences by late April or early May. On the return journey, starting in July, most rufous hummingbirds turn inland and take the scenic route to Mexico via the Rocky Mountains, although the route appears to change depending on age and gender. Recently, the migratory routes of this declining species have also been affected by habitat loss and climate change.

Each journey takes the little birds several months, so they prepare every time by fattening up before they leave. They migrate in many stages, though, regularly dropping in on their favourite flowers to top up their energy levels as they travel.

Rufous hummingbirds have excellent memories and often return to the exact same flowering plants along their migratory routes year after year.

LEATHERBACK SEA TURTLE

Leatherback sea turtles are the largest turtles on Earth and can grow to around two metres long. Unlike others that have hard shells, these turtles have leathery, almost rubbery shells. They can be found in tropical and temperate waters such as the Atlantic, Pacific and Indian oceans.

These turtles undertake the longest migration of any sea turtle, travelling about 6000 kilometres between their coastal breeding grounds and ocean feeding grounds each year, and then back again.

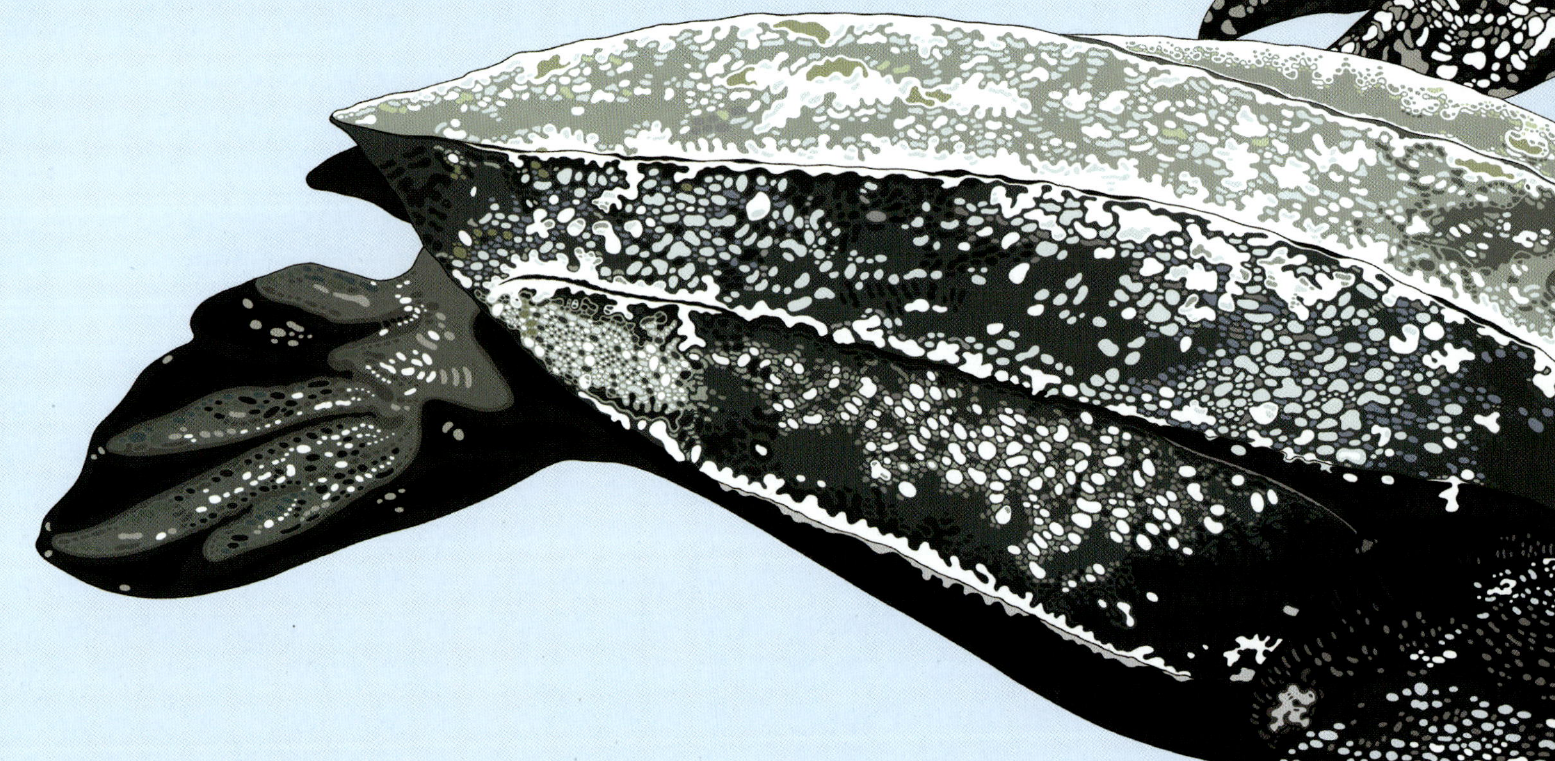

Between their annual migration and their constant search for jellyfish to eat, leatherback sea turtles can swim up to 16 000 kilometres in one year.

After mating, the males remain at sea while the females come ashore to nest. In a single night, the females build their nests in the sand, then lay and bury their eggs to protect them. They usually lay around 80–100 eggs in one go. This is known as a clutch. The females lay many clutches in different nests during nesting season.

The baby turtles, called hatchlings, are barely five centimetres long when they emerge from their shells. The hatchlings must dig their way out of the sand before immediately scurrying towards the ocean. Many are scooped up by waiting sea birds before they reach the water's edge. For those that make it to the ocean, large fish are usually waiting for their own easy meal.

For the lucky few hatchlings that make it safely beyond their first few months, a long life of roaming the world's oceans awaits. When the females reach maturity at around 15–20 years old, they migrate back to the area where they hatched to breed and lay their own eggs. The males spend their whole lives at sea.

BOGONG MOTH

The bogong moth may look perfectly ordinary at first glance but is, in fact, a vital Australian species. It is both a food source for many animals and a pollinator for the many native plants the moths visit on their annual migration.

This migration begins in spring in the dry, inland plains of south-eastern Australia, when young adult moths emerge from the ground where they have spent winter as caterpillars. Up to two thousand million moths travel around 1000 kilometres south to find caves and crannies in the Australian Alps, where they will hibernate over summer.

Amazingly, with only one migration in their short lives, the young moths know exactly where to go.

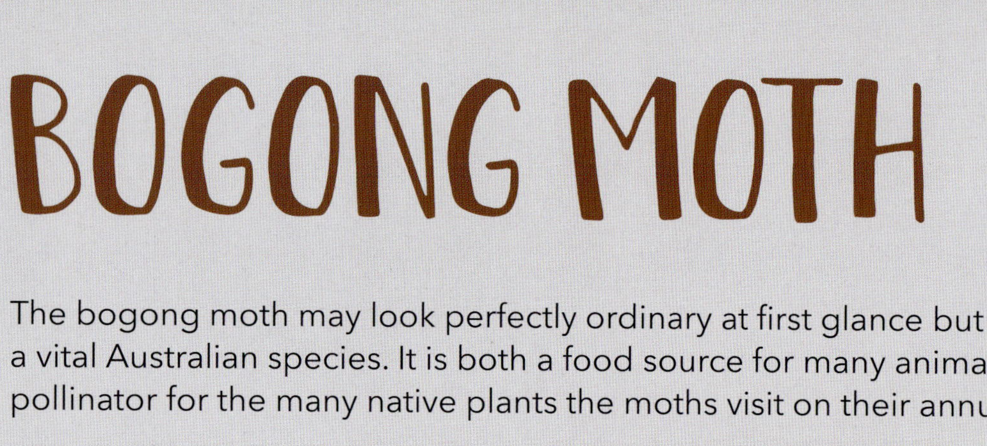

They spend their days hidden away and travel by night, stopping regularly to feed on nectar to build up the fat reserves they'll need to survive their summer hibernation.

Unlike most animals that migrate for food or to breed, bogong moths migrate to find somewhere cool and sheltered from the harsh Australian summer. At the end of the season, they return to their breeding grounds, where the cycle begins all over again.

In the past, the moths created an impressive spectacle in caves, stacked up on top of each other and packed in tightly, with as many as 17 000 moths in a single square metre. In recent years, this once abundant moth has lost over 99 per cent of its population, believed to be caused by drought in their breeding areas as well as land-clearing, the use of pesticides, light pollution that disrupts their sense of direction, and climate change.

A NOTE ON CONSERVATION AND CLIMATE CHANGE

In reading this book, you may have been delighted to learn of the incredible journeys these animals undertake but also sad to read about the great dangers they face along the way. As the author, I felt both these emotions throughout the writing process.

I was constantly amazed by how some animals know where to travel with no one to show them, such as the young cuckoos and monarch butterflies. Or how others can fly for days at a time without rest, like the bar-tailed godwit, or swim across entire oceans for years and still find their way back to where they were born, like sea turtles and salmon.

But I was saddened, too, as I learned how human activity and climate change are affecting the ability of many animals to migrate. This not only has negative consequences for the animal itself but can have a ripple effect on other animals, plants and whole ecosystems.

Climate change is one of the most talked about issues today, which is not surprising given the great impact it is having on our planet. While specific predictions change as our knowledge increases, there is now global scientific consensus that climate change is happening fast and that it is driven by human activity.

Climate change is warming the planet: deserts are expanding, wetlands are drying, and the ice in the Arctic and Antarctica is melting. This global warming is disrupting weather patterns, causing more floods, more storms and more bushfires. All these things make it harder and harder for animals to survive, and this can be especially true for animals that travel long distances. Some migrating animals have had to change their routes or destinations as their usual habitats become hotter, drier or more flood-prone, giving them less time to breed, feed and travel. For many, keeping up with climate change is just not possible, and those species are becoming endangered.

The caribou are a clear example of this. The warming of their Arctic homes has led to them migrating earlier each year. This leads to them giving birth earlier, which leaves the calves more vulnerable to the drastically changing weather patterns of the Arctic. The survival rate of baby caribou is falling.

Another example from the Arctic is how milder winters are causing lemming numbers to fall. Lemmings used to be the main food source for Arctic foxes, so this has led to hungry foxes eating the eggs and chicks of migratory sea birds such as the bar-tailed godwit instead. In this example, it's easy to see the ripple effect of climate change in action.

Humans are negatively impacting animal migrations in other ways too. Habitat loss, when human activity encroaches on the spaces animals need to survive, can disrupt or even completely prevent traditional migration patterns. Sadly, every animal in this book is affected by habitat loss to some degree.

Land-clearing is a major cause of habitat loss and a global problem of huge proportions. All over the world, land is being cleared for mines, to produce more meat and wood, and to build more cities and more roads. When this impacts the homes or migration routes of animals, those animals can become endangered or be pushed to extinction. In Australia, swift parrots are still losing their homes despite being critically endangered, while in Central Asia the saiga antelope is finding its traditional migration routes blocked by fences built along country borders. These obstacles, combined with illegal hunting, disease and increasing drought due to climate change, leave the saiga antelope with nowhere to go.

Some of the species in this book are small, seemingly insignificant creatures, like the bogong moth. But sometimes these tiny creatures can have a huge impact. In the case of the bogong moth, rapidly declining moth numbers are contributing to the loss of other animals and plant species, in particular the endangered mountain pygmy possum, which relies on the moth as a source of food.

Despite what sounds like endless bad news, there are many people and organisations around the world working hard to help migrating animals. On Christmas Island, locals have built roadside barriers and special crab bridges over busy roads to help lessen the impact of humans on the migrating Christmas Island red crabs. Across Africa, wildlife conservation groups work with landowners and local communities to keep migration routes open for wildebeest and zebras, whose migratory paths are increasingly blocked by fences. On beaches in many parts of the world, local conservation groups patrol the shore when leatherback sea turtles hatch to help more of this threatened species survive on their way to the seashore. And scientists in Tasmania have built dozens of specially designed nesting boxes for swift parrots who can't find a suitable hollow tree for nesting. In many different countries, scientists are studying the effects of climate change on animals so we can learn how to better protect them.

The situation may look bleak and fixing these problems may seem a huge task, but there is a role for all of us to play, even if we are small. For example, people who live on the migration path of the rufous hummingbird have been planting trees and flowers that these hummingbirds need to feed on – we can do the same for birds and insects in our own region. We can eat less meat and dairy products to reduce the need for land-clearing, and we can learn about sustainable seafood to ensure our eating habits are not harming the ocean and the many species, like the Pacific bluefin tuna, that live there. By learning more, and sharing our knowledge with family and friends, we all become more aware of how our lives affect animals, their habitats and their migration routes.

Another easy and important way we can help is by collecting rubbish any time we go to the beach so that migrating leatherback sea turtles don't accidentally eat plastic instead of jellyfish. And because all the plastic ever made still exists today, and won't decompose for another five hundred years, we can avoid introducing yet more plastic into our environment by using sustainable alternatives. Instead of buying plastic water bottles or plastic toothbrushes, for example, we can carry reusable water bottles and brush our teeth using toothbrushes made of bamboo. Just don't forget to turn off the tap to save water while you brush!

There are so many different ways we can help our planet become a better place for animals and humans alike. Let's work together to make a difference, do our best for the animals and create a healthier, happier world for us all!

GLOSSARY

chrysalis	the hard outside covering of a moth or butterfly that protects it while it grows into an adult with wings
clutch	a group of eggs laid at one time in the same nest
colonies	groups of animals, of the same kind, that live together
krill	tiny crustaceans, the diet of the humpback whale
larvae	the very young form of certain animals including dragonflies and other insects, as well as eels, crabs and frogs
monogamous	having only one mate
poaching	illegally hunting, trapping or fishing
pollinate	the process of moving pollen to fertilise plants
spawn	the act of fish, frogs, crabs, insects and other creatures producing a large number of eggs directly into water
spawning grounds	the area where an animal spawns
steppes	broad and dry grassy plains of south-western Russia and Central Asia
tundra	vast, flat, treeless plains of the Arctic regions of Europe, Asia and North America
wetlands	land such as marshes and swamps where the soil is thoroughly wet

RESOURCES

I hope you feel inspired to read more and learn more. There is so much information out there on all the animals in this book, as well as other animals, their habitats and the environment we all share. In researching this book, I used many different sources. My key sources are listed below.

All About Birds   https://www.allaboutbirds.org/news
Australian Geographic   https://www.australiangeographic.com.au
Australian Museum   https://australian.museum
BBC Earth   https://www.bbcearth.com
Birdlife Australia   https://birdlife.org.au
Fact Animal   https://factanimal.com
National Geographic   https://www.nationalgeographic.com
National Geographic Kids   https://kids.nationalgeographic.com/animals
Our Breathing Planet   https://www.ourbreathingplanet.com
World Land Trust   https://www.worldlandtrust.org
World Wildlife Fund   https://www.worldwildlife.org

ABOUT THE AUTHOR

Jennifer Cossins is a CBCA award-winning artist and writer with a passion for nature, the animal kingdom and all things bright and colourful. A born and bred Tasmanian, Jennifer also designs homewares, textiles and stationery, which she stocks in her store in Hobart, Red Parka. Jennifer's other books include *A–Z of Endangered Animals*, *101 Collective Nouns*, *The Baby Animal Book*, *A–Z of Australian Animals*, *The Ultimate Animal Counting Book*, *A Flamboyance of Flamingos*, *The Mummy Animal Book*, *The Daddy Animal Book*, *The Ultimate Animal Alphabet Book* and *Book of Curious Birds*.